FOOD AROUND THE WORLD

Food in Italy

Polly Goodman

PowerKiDS press.

New York

Published in 2008 by The Rosen Publishing Group, Inc.
29 East 21st Street, New York, NY 10010

First Edition

Editor: Sarah Gay
Senior Design Manager: Rosamund Saunders
Designer: Tim Mayer
Consultant: Susannah Blake

Library of Congress Cataloging-in-Publication Data

Goodman, Polly.
  Food in Italy / Polly Goodman. — 1st ed.
     p. cm. — (Food around the world)
  Includes index.
  ISBN 978-1-4042-4298-2 (library binding)
  1. Cookery, Italian—Juvenile literature. 2. Food habits—Italy—Juvenile literature. I. Title.
  TX723.G6296 2008
  641.5945—dc22
                                    2007032610

Manufactured in China

Cover photograph: a delicatessen in Piedmont, northern Italy.

Photo credits: Glenn Beanland/Lonely Planet 6, Dallas Stribley/Lonely Planet 8, John and Lisa Merrill/Danita Delimont 9, Frank Weider/Photolibrary 10, Peter Williams/Anthony Blake Photo Library 11, CuboImages srl/Alamy 12, 20, 23 and 24, Rawdon Wyatt/Anthony Blake Photo Library 13, Alan Benson/Lonely Planet 14 and 15, Robert Frerck/Getty Images 16, Rocco Fasano/Lonely Planet 17 and title page, Norman Hollands/Anthony Blake Photo Library 18, Juliet Coombe/Lonely Planet 19, ACE STOCK LIMITED/Alamy 21, Donald C Landwehrle/Getty Images 22, SIME/Dutton Colin/4corners Images 25, Karl Newedel/Getty Images 26, Stephen Saks/Lonely Planet cover.

Contents

Welcome to Italy   6

Farming and weather   8

Wheat, corn, and rice   10

Fruit and vegetables   12

Meat, fish, and cheese   14

Shopping for food   16

Mealtimes in Italy   18

Around the country   20

Special occasions   22

Festival food   24

Make Insalata Caprese!   26

A balanced diet   27

Glossary   28

Further information and Web Sites   29

Index   30

Words in **bold** can be found in the glossary on page 28

Welcome to Italy

Italy is a long, narrow country in Southern Europe. Italian cooking has been famous since **Roman times**. Italy is well known for its pizza, pasta, and ice cream, which are eaten all around the world, but there are lots of other delicious Italian foods, too.

▼ *Olives from Italian olive* **groves** *are sold in shops all over the world.*

▲ *Italy and the Italian islands are marked in orange on this map.*

Farming and weather

Italy stretches from the Alps in the north to the Mediterranean Sea in the south. Some foods grow well in Southern Italy, where it is hot and dry. Other foods grow better in the north, where it is cooler and wetter than the south.

▼ *Farmers* **harvest** *their crops on the island of Sardinia.*

In the north, the main crops are wheat and rice. **Dairy** cows graze in the mountains and in the **fertile** river valleys. In the south, fruits such as oranges and lemons, and many different vegetables, ripen easily in the hot sun.

▲ Grapes are grown all over Italy. They can be made into wine.

Wheat, corn, and rice

Wheat and corn are Italy's most important crops. Wheat is made into different breads, such as **ciabatta**, **focaccia**, and **grissini**, as well as cakes, pizza bases, and pasta.

◀ Bruschetta is toasted bread with garlic, salt and pepper, olive oil, and sometimes other ingredients, such as tomatoes.

Food fact
There are over 50 different shapes of pasta, such as spaghetti, macaroni, lasagne, and ravioli.

Pasta is made by mixing flour, eggs, and salt into a dough and cutting it into shapes. Corn is ground to make **polenta**. Rice is made into risotto, a creamy dish from Northern Italy.

▲ *This chef is making sheets of pasta called lasagne.*

Fruit and vegetables

Fresh fruits and vegetables, such as tomatoes and olives, are important in Italian cooking. Tomatoes are used in salads, sauces, pizza toppings, and soups. Olives are **marinated** or made into olive oil.

◄ Insalata caprese *is a salad from Capri, made with mozzarella, tomato, and basil. You can find the recipe on page 26.*

Grapes are grown in every region and can be made into wine. Fresh cherries, apricots, peaches, and plums are eaten after meals, or made into delicious desserts like *cassata alla siciliana* (an ice cream from Sicily).

▼ *Basil leaves are ground with a* **pestle** *and* **mortar** *to make pesto sauce.*

Food fact

Pesto is a famous sauce made from basil leaves, garlic, pine nuts, and olive oil.

Meat, fish, and cheese

Veal, beef, and ham are the most popular types of meat in Italy. Minced beef is used in pasta sauces. Ham is either served fresh, or **cured** like salami and **prosciutto**.

◀ *Carpaccio is enjoyed all over Italy. It is marinated, raw beef sliced very thinly.*

Food fact
Italians use cow's milk, sheep's milk, and even buffalo milk to make all kinds of cheese.

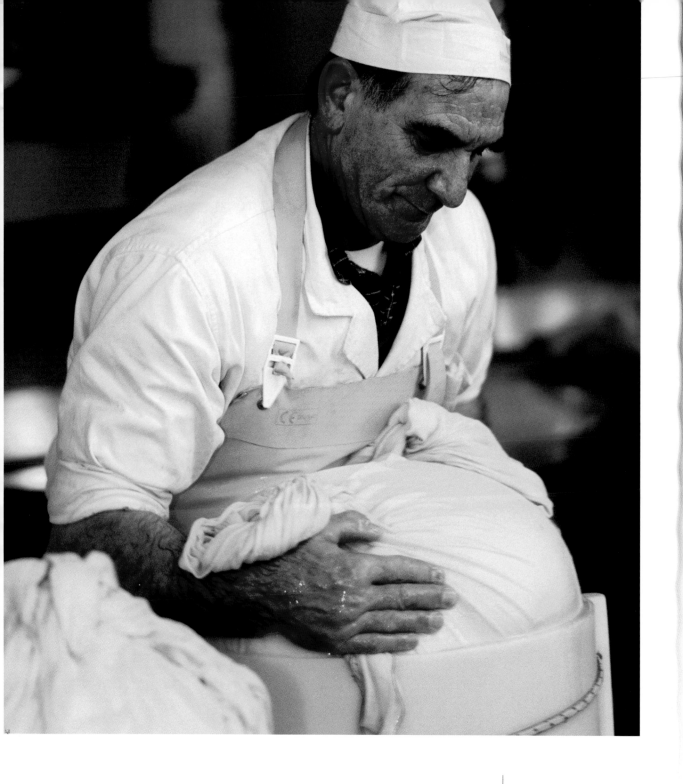

Sardines, anchovies, swordfish, and shellfish are fished from the Mediterranean and Adriatic seas. Trout, carp, and perch are caught in lakes and rivers. Fish is grilled, made into soup, or cooked in pasta sauces.

▲ *This man is making some Parmesan cheese by putting it into a mold.*

Shopping for food

Almost every village, town, and city in Italy has a daily market that sells fresh fruit, vegetables, and meat from local farms. People buy the freshest food available, which changes from season to season.

▼ Oranges, lemons, and nuts are for sale at an Italian fruit market.

Most towns have a **panetteria**, which sells bread and cakes, and a general store called an *alimentari*. Some towns also have pasta shops called *pastifichio*.

▲ *This pasta shop in Naples sells every type of pasta.*

Mealtimes in Italy

Everyday Italian meals might include dishes from the menus below.

Breakfast

Crostini (little toasts)

Sweet biscuit or *brioche* (cake)

___

Coffee

Lunch

Antipasti including salami, stuffed peppers, and artichokes

___

▲ *This plate of antipasti includes Parma ham, salami, artichokes, olives, and sundried tomatoes.*

Lunch

Soup or pasta

Meat or fish dish
Vegetables
Salad

Fresh fruit
Cheese

Coffee espresso

Dinner

Pasta
Fresh vegetables

Coffee

▼ Hot, roasted chestnuts from a street vendor make a tasty snack.

Around the country

Different regions and cities in Italy are known for different types of food. The northern region of Lombardy is famous for its mascarpone and gorgonzola cheeses.

▼ *Cassata is a delicious cake from Sicily.*

Many dishes are named after the places where they were first made. *Spaghetti alla Bolognese* comes from the city of Bologna. Parma ham and Parmesan cheese come from the city of Parma.

▲ Pizza was first cooked in Naples.

Special occasions

Italians celebrate important events with feasts. At an Italian wedding, up to fourteen different courses are served. Sugared almonds, called *confetti*, are put on the table beside each place.

◀ *Every Italian wedding has a cake covered with icing or fresh cream.*

22

Many towns celebrate a good **harvest** with a festival. The town of Aqualanga has a **truffle** festival, where truffles are hunted with pigs and donkeys. In Viterbo, there is a cherry festival with parades and dancing. People eat delicious cherry desserts.

▲ In Ivrea, a yearly orange battle helps people to remember an ancient fight against an evil lord.

Festival food

Most Italians are Roman Catholics, and their most important festival is Holy Week, or Easter. On Good Friday, people take part in street processions. On Easter Sunday, families get together for a special dinner of feast breads, Easter pies, and chocolate eggs.

▼ *This Easter pie is made from over 18 layers of pastry, **ricotta** cheese, and whole eggs.*

Forty days before Easter, people eat up the last rich foods before **Lent**. Italians celebrate by going to street parades and eating deep-fried pastries dusted with sugar. In Florence, people eat *schiacciata di carnevale*, a special carnival cake.

▼ *In the Viareggio Carnival parade, children throw candies to the crowds from huge papier-mâché puppets.*

Make Insalata Caprese!

What you need

4 ½ oz. (125 g)
mozzarella
2 large tomatoes
12 fresh basil leaves
extra virgin olive oil
salt and pepper

What to do

1. Drain the liquid from the mozzarella and slice it thinly.
2. Slice the tomatoes.
3. Arrange the mozzarella, tomato slices, and basil on a serving plate.
4. Drizzle with a little olive oil, season with salt and pepper, and serve.

Ask an adult to help you make this salad, and always be careful with sharp knives.

A balanced diet

This food pyramid shows which foods you should eat to have a healthy, **balanced diet**.

We shouldn't eat too many fats, oils, cakes, and candies.

Milk, cheese, meat, fish, beans, and eggs help to keep us strong.

We should eat plenty of vegetables and fruit to keep healthy.

Bread, cereal, rice, and pasta should make up most of our diet.

Italian meals use all foods from the pyramid. They are usually quite healthy, because they are mostly made up of pasta or bread with fruit and vegetables, as well as some fish, meat, and cheese.

Glossary

antipasti hot and cold dishes served as a first course

ciabatta a soft bread shaped like a slipper. "Ciabatta" is the Italian word for "slippper."

crops plants grown for food

cured when meat is salted to make it last longer

dairy anything to do with milk

delicatessen a shop selling cooked meats, cheeses, and local foods

fertile land that is good for growing crops

focaccia a flat, dimpled bread sprinkled with olive oil and salt

grissini crunchy bread sticks from Piedmont

groves a small wood or planting of fruit trees

harvest to gather a crop

Lent the period of 40 days before Easter

marinated soaked in a savory sauce to add flavor

mortar a bowl used to pound or grind foods in, such as herbs

panetteria a bakery

pestle a club-shaped kitchen tool used for pounding and grinding foods, such as herbs

polenta a porridge made from corn cooked in salted water

prosciutto cured (salted) ham

ricotta a white cheese

Roman times the ancient Romans ruled Italy and much of Europe for over 1,000 years, from 509 B.C. until A.D. 476

truffles a type of underground mushroom

Further information

Books to read

A World of Recipes: Italy by Julie McCulloch (Heinemann, 2001)

Festive Foods and Celebrations: Italian Foods and Culture
by Jennifer Ferro (Rourke Publishing, 1999)

*Kids Around the World Celebrate!: The Best Feasts and Festivals from
Many Lands* by Lynda Jones (Jossey-Bass, 1999)

Let's Eat! What Children Eat Around the World by Beatrice Hollyer
(Henry Holt and Co, 2004)

Letters from Around the World: Italy by Fiona Tankard
(Cherrytree Books, 2002)

Picture a Country: Italy by Henry Pluckrose (Franklin Watts, 1998)

Web Sites
Due to the changing nature of Internet links, PowerKids Press has developed an online list of Web sites
related to the subject of this book. This site is regularly updated. Please use this link to access this list:
www.powerkidslinks.com/faw/italy

Index

All the numbers in **bold** refer to photographs.

A
antipasti   18, **18**

B
breads   10, **10**, 17, 24, 27
breakfast   18

C
cakes   17, 18, 20, **20**, 22, **22**, 25
Capri   12
carnival   25, **25**
cheeses   12, 14, 15, **15**, 17, 19, 20, 21, 24, **24**, 26, **26**, 27
coffee   19
corn   10, 11
crops   9, 10

D
dinner   19, 24

E
Easter   24
eggs   24, **24**

F
fruits   9, **9**, 12–13, 16, **16**, 19, 20, **20**, 23, **23**, 27

H
harvest   8, **8**, 23

I
ice creams   6, 13, 20, **20**

L
lunch   19

M
market   16, **16**
meat   14, **14**, 17, 18, **18**, 21, 27

P
pasta   6, 10–11, **11**, 15, 17, **17**, 19, 21, 27
pesto   **13**
pizzas   6, 10, 12, 21, **21**
polenta   11

R
rice   9, 11
risotto   10

S
salads   12, **12**, 26, **26**
sauces   13, **13**, 14, 15
seafoods   15, 27
shops   16–17, **17**
Sicily   7, 13
soups   12, 15, 19

T
truffles   23

V
vegetables   9, 12–13, 19, 26, **26**, 27

W
weather   8
weddings   22, **22**
wheat   8, **8**–9, 10
wines   9, 13